ABOUT THE AUTHOR

Born in Derby but based in Manchester, Rory moves between the worlds of poetry, music and theatre. A former teacher and youth worker, Rory was a part of the BBC New Creatives scheme in 2020, and is currently part of South Bank's 2022 New Poets Collective. Rory has published his first collection with Bearded Badger press. His first two person show 'This Town' was showcased at Contact & Derby Theatre in March 2023. The narrative poem which formed the basis of this show is *And within these cobbled streets,* published by VERVE Poetry Press at the same time.

ABOUT *THIS TOWN*:

COMMISSIONED BY CONTACT AND DERBY THEATRE. SUPPORTED BY PUBLIC FUNDING BY THE NATIONAL LOTTERY THROUGH ARTS COUNCIL ENGLAND.

"This is for those from the far-off towns that nobody's heard of. Who sit on busses rolling backwards out of cities and watch everything fall into silence."

This Town is a modern-day epic narrative poem, performed and written by exciting new talent Rory Aaron (BBC New Creatives, Southbank Poetry Collective). *This Town* is based on Rory's original narrative poem, *And within these cobbled streets*, recently published by VERVE Poetry Press.

An ode to home, *This Town* uses powerful spoken word to transport us to a post-industrialised landscape, weaving together stories of loss, PTSD, and friendship.

This Town is based on Rory's original narrative poem, *And within these cobbled streets*, recently published by VERVE Poetry Press.

Written and Performed by: Rory Aaron
Director: Cheryl Martin
Producer: Roxy Moores for Contact
Performer: Kate Ireland
Composer: Blythe Pepino
Movement Director: Chris Brown

Contact, Oxford Rd, Manchester   Mar 22 - Mar 30 2023
Derby Theatre, St Peter's Quarter, Derby   Apr 1 2023

Rory Aaron
And within these cobbled streets

VERVE
POETRY PRESS
BIRMINGHAM

PUBLISHED BY VERVE POETRY PRESS
https://vervepoetrypress.com
mail@vervepoetrypress.com

All rights reserved
© 2023 Rory Aaron

The right of Rory Aaron to be identified as author of this work has been asserted in accordance with section 77 of the Copyright, Designs and Patents Act 1988.

No part of this work may be reproduced, stored or transmitted in any form or by any means, graphic, electronic, recorded or mechanical, without the prior written permission of the publisher.

FIRST PUBLISHED MARCH 2023

Printed and bound in the UK
by ImprintDigital, Exeter

ISBN: 978-1-913917-28-9

To my partner Leigh

And within these cobbled streets

I

This Town
with its cobbled streets and terraced houses.
Its back alleys filled with trodden autumn leaves
and McDonald's receipts. Its old family names etched
into the stones of cemeteries
and kids laughing and playing the monkey bars.
Whilst teenagers are necking skittles and vodka
after dark. It's the corner shop, where little'uns
buy footie stickers to fill their mags,
and they still don't charge you for plastic bags.
It's chippy next to the Chinese and the plastic
seats on the 63. Its shadows of the old Victorian
chimneys that catch the heels of your feet
as you walk down past the great North Mill
that is empty but still stands like the castle
it once was. Blood stained walls and cracked
windows, the echoes of God knows how many voices.
Great brothers. Great sisters. Great aunties. Great uncles.
All sit within its spider's web. Its metallic structure.
Its energy propelled by Derwent water.
A target during the war ya know lad.
We once made bolts for all those northern factories.
But we never get credit for that, grandads say
to their grandkids, who cross their grandkids in the street.
You see this town is a town you never leave.

*

Unless you're Dean.
Who we find standing outside The Rifleman's,
still slightly knobbly kneed dressed in skinny jeans,
frame hung like the awkward teen he once was.
Except now, Dean's 25. And Dean's got a degree.
Alongside a decent salary. He doesn't own a house,
but does live down south, with his girlfriend
in a small flat in Hackney.
But he's not been back here in time.
About seven years to be precise. So as he steps
inside through the wooden doors
he feels his footsteps tap out their own irrelevance.
In his head he is practising his opening sentences.
Nervous about the sentiments, those old decrepit
elephants that could fill the room.
But luckily for Dean, the room smells just as it used to.
Stale Carling and cigarettes. Salt and vinegar crisps
and Scotch whis- *Oi posh lad* - Dean turns his head.
And there's Joe. Sat at a table with two pints
and three battered beer mats.
Joe doesn't stand but does extend the right hand.
Skin slightly tanned from working on the land.
Joe didn't become a student. No Joe didn't do that.
His shoulders built like the width of the Berlin wall
hair cut short, muscles firm and taught, knuckles jagged
like javelins. *Long time no see lad*, he says,
gripping Deans hand. *How've you been?*

II

Behind The Rifleman's there is this jitty.
Here are Dean and Joe dressed like scallies
aged fifteen in TN Shox and trackies baggy.
With one BMX and one rusty Raleigh.
The stars are hidden. The clouds are thick.
A wind is blowing. The street lights are lit.
The jitty is about four elbows wide.
Joe's looking left and right. Deans crouched,
down by the wall, a half lit cigarette in his left,
a marker pen in his right. *Fuck off.* He goes for
one exclamation mark, all of it underlined.
Oi, what's the time? asks Joe.
About 7:15, Dean replies. *What time do you have
to be home tonight? Anytime*, says Joe. *My Mum's
still working nights. Same*, says Dean.
My brother gets back tonight.
Right, says Joe. *Where has he been this time?*
Iraq, says Dean. Joe doesn't know
what to say, so looks up to the sky, where a flock
of pigeons are on the move and a star is peaking through.
In the distance there is the sound of two lorries rumbling.
He climbs on the wall of the jitty to take a look.
One Eddie Stobart. Followed by one TNT. Both lorries
that his dad used to drive. Joe closes his eyes,
and remembers those long summers
where he would go with him.

They'd drive from Derby to Aberdeen,
bunkering down on blow up beds, in the car parks
of service stations. He'd sleep locked between his dad's
forearms, knowing that no harm could come to him.
And during the day, he'd sit behind the wheel
on his dad's knees, windows open feeling the breeze
he'd sing Bruce Springsteen, at the top of his lungs.
He'd feel free. *They're here*, says Dean.
Joe, drops down from the wall, feels his feet
hit the floor, and pushes those memories aside.
On the opposite side of the jitty, two silhouettes
appear through the mist. It's Luke and Alex.
Everything goes silent. And for a moment
Joe feels like they're in a scene
from one of those old western flicks. The type
that his dad used to sit and watch on a Sunday
with the curtains drawn, and a stiff drink.

III

It's morning now, and Joe is looking out
the window. His fists are bruised and scuffed
his t-shirt torn up on the floor. The sun has risen.
The birds are singing. He needs to leave.
If he doesn't he will miss the bus to school.
His report will go from amber to red.
The deputy head will call his Mum. She will cry
and they will fight. He lies back on his bed. Takes a breath.
He places both his hands behind his head.
The image of last night comes back.
The sound of clashing fists. Cracking chin.
Snapping ribs. Neck gripped. Nails digged.
Piecing skin. Throwing Luke down on the floor.
Blood stained on the jitty wall.
How the rain started to fall.
That's enough, he thinks.
The fight is won. What's done is done.
Boys scrapping is ancient
and he won't be the first. Or the last.
It could have been worse, he thinks.
He could have lost. He lies back on the bed.
Pulls his knees up to his chest, clamps his eyes shut
and doesn't move until he hears the bus for school.
The low rumble of its engine.
The screeching of the brakes. The hiss
of the hydraulic door. The chatter

from the bottom floor. *Ah fuck it*, he thinks. *Fuck the teachers. Fuck Dean who ran. Fuck Jessie. She will ask too many questions. Like what happened to your face? Or why are your firsts all torn and bruised? And what's that mark on your shoes?* He doesn't move, until he is sure the bus has pulled off from the stop. Then he stands, grabs his bag. But not the one for school.

IV

Joe enters through the doors. The gym is old.
Cold stone walls painted white. No music plays.
Just the sound of cast iron and stainless steel.
The clanging of weights. Long florescent tubes of light
and the smell of sweat, chalk and dust. Sarah
is behind the desk. She has brown hair, plucked eyebrows,
a perma tan and red lipstick. An old picture of her is framed
on the counter. Skin tanned, teeth bright and white.
Muscles flexed. *You wouldn't mess with her*, thinks Joe,
even now ten years later. Alright Joe. She says,
Alright Sarah, he replies,
Vlad is in the back, says Sarah.
Vlad is her husband, he's tall and strong
with boxers arms. Newspaper cuttings
line the wall, of all the different fights he won.

Why aren't you at school?
asks Vlad, as Joe slings his bag
onto the changing room floor.
Couldn't be bothered, shrugs Joe.
Didn't want the trouble. Vlad looks him
up and down. Clocks his face. Clocks his hands.
Clocks his shoes. He can guess what has happened.
But he doesn't say anything. Who is he to judge?

Come on, says Vlad, as they leave the changing
room together. *Just strap up your fists.*
And in the back, there's some gloves with extra padding.
Go get them, then start working the bag.
Jab. Cross. Hook. Cross.
Joe loves it here in the gym. Where everything is still
and mist rises from his lips.
Left. Right. Hook Jab.
It's here where he can think most clearly
about his dad.
How a man he loved could leave him just like that.
Left. Right. Hook Jab.
One day here. Another day gone.
Change, shouts Vlad.
Joe picks up the skipping rope, into press ups,
into burpees into jumping jacks,
then back onto the bags.
It's now been six years since he last saw his dad.
He left hooks the bag, drops the shoulders,
then mimics working the body.
Good, says Vlad. *Three weeks till your fight.*
Imagine five hundred eyes watching your every move.
Hear the cheers, feel the boo's. Allow your heart
to beat every time you move your feet. Stay in control.
Stay focused. Be patient. One clean blow and this lad
will fall. One clean blow that's all you need.
But Joe is breathing heavy now, sweat streaming down
his face. Pain grips his body as he beats
it black and blue. Pushing himself further
into the darkness into a world where he can twist
himself in two, and make his body feel
everything he feels. He wants to scream

but keeps it in. Vlad stands back watching him.
He recognises everything.
Nice one, he says. *Good session. Go take
a shower young man.*

V

Dean stares down at the school desk. He's sat in French.
Again. And none of it makes any sense.
The different words, the strange way they use tense.
It hurts his head. So he takes his pen,
and with his tongue touching his lips, he draws
a very simple cross on top of his index finger tip.
Jessie laughs and shakes her head. Dean smiles
and takes a breath. He can feel her presence,
all over his body. It's the way she crosses her legs,
and ties her hair back revealing her neck.
It's her smile. Her lips. The cool badges she has stitched
on her black rucksack. How she can drop in
on a half pipe, play bass guitar, and ride no handed
on her bike. *I'm in love with you*, Dean wants to say,
but never does. Instead he just goes red,
then looks away and feels the goosebumps
tiptoe down his neck. He stares at the window,
and leans back in his seat. He wants to crack a joke.
See a smile cause those dimples in her cheeks.
But before he can he feels her nudge his arm.
What, he mouths. She nods to the front of the class.
Dean looks. Mr Kent is staring at him.
Arms folded around his chest. Eyebrows
so high they're touching his hairline.
Did you not hear what I said?

No, says Dean, panicking and staring at the board.
What the fuck does Je m'applle mean?
I was miles away. The whole class laughs.
Clearly, says Mr Kent, *but you're needed at reception.
A message has just come through.*
Dean shrugs and tries to play it cool.
He slowly stands, packs his books into his Nike
drawstring bag. Hands Jessie her spare pen back
before walking out of class.

The reception is in the North Block.
Up the jitty. Left at the gates. Then down the drive.
Everything is concrete. Except for the fences,
which are green with tall and deadly spikes.
Pigeons poke around the potholes,
and gangs of seagulls gather, collars popped,
in the centre of the netless tennis courts.
Beneath a dark grey
sky two empty buses sit, as the caretaker
pushes a cart filled with paint past
a row of deserted portacabins
that look depressed. Dean turns left,
past the canteen The smell of fried bacon
floats out the kitchen where the dinner ladies
are working hard. Eventually he arrives.
The doors slide open and to his surprise,
there's his brother. He looks tired,
clothes hanging off his frame
like they didn't before. His face is thin.
Withdrawn. Shoulders hunched.
He looks up from the floor.
Alright Dean, he says.

Alright bro, Dean replies,
Fancy going for some lunch?
Ye sure. Why not? Have the school said I can?
He glances up at the receptionist who nods.
They leave the school. Turn right.
Head to Park Farm, where old ladies push
trolleys past dodgy electronic shops,
and on the corner there is a George's
fish and chip shop. They order a large chips
two cans of coke, find some seats
in the corner. *It's been a while*, says his brother.
It has, says Dean, pushing his feet into the floor.
How you've been since I left? Alright? Up to no good?
What's this about you smoking?
How come you're back? Dean interrupts. *I thought you had
another three months.* His brother looks up. Dean stares
into his eyes. They don't look good. They seem
vacant, darker. Like they've seen something he doesn't
want to share. *Have you killed someone?* Asks Dean,
putting a chip into his mouth. Liam smiles,
glances at his brother. Even though it's only been
a couple months, he looks taller, older. A little broader.
His voice has dropped, some baby fluff
has appeared beneath his nose.
Liam goes to open his mouth.
He wants to tell Dean about the seizures,
and how he wakes up shaking,
unable to breathe, with a ringing
in his ears. One minute he's acting normal,
the next he's being picked up off the floor.
He plays with the salt shaker.
Picks up a chip. Dips it in the ketchup.

I'm just back, he says instead, *I want to be around.*
Dean nods his head, *Cool. Cool. Ye that sounds cool*
Nothing much else is said. They eat their chips
in silence. Lick the grease from their fingertips.
Crush their cans. Flick through sport pages,
pause at the football and speak
about the different scores, before Dean
heads off back to school.

VI

In the pub, Liam sits alone, staring
at his half empty pint. He taps his fingers
on the table tries to ignore the ringing in his ears,
before picking up the glass, and knocking it back.
He nods at Clara, asks for another.
With a shot of vodka on the side. *Nice one.*
He knows he shouldn't, but what else is there to do?
In truth. He hates it here.
Last night he wandered the streets,
climbed the steps of the tallest bridge,
stared at the empty road below,
watched as the cats eyes copied the stars.
It's the fresh smell of the air. How there's no stench
of burning diesel. No fear of snipers
as tar melts beneath your boots,
as you stand plastic handle of your rifle gripped.
Another routine patrol sweeping the roads
checking for IEDs. He stands, picks up the pint
and shot sits back down,
and lets his mind fall back,
to where he's been. Basra. Basra.
Venice of the East, where wood carved Shanasheel
cast shadows down crumbling ancient streets.
Where bombed out yachts sink slowly into the river.
A Ferris wheel spins on the bank,
and kids sit on the back of open trucks whilst

rockets light up the sky over the palace.
In the army they teach you how to measure distance
from the size of torsos, to know every kilometre
is roughly six hundred steps, to squeeze the trigger
and follow through like it's your final breath.
But now his ears won't stop ringing.
And on his Blackberry there's an email
claiming he's unfit for future service.
So what does he do? The vodka stings his throat.
His vision goes blurred. Nobody died.
He tells himself again. *Nobody died.*
But that screaming flash of light. Distorted space.
Cloud of dust. Legs collapsing
on a road walked a thousand times before.
Fire and smoke chewing up his lungs.
When an IED explodes, everything moves slow.
For a moment he thought he had died.
Until he heard this ringing. *Nobody died*,
he says again. *Nobody died.*

A hand appears on his shoulder.
He looks up. A group of lads stand around him,
that he knew from when he was young.
Alright Liam, they say. *When did you get back?
How many did you kill this time?*
Liam tries to laugh and offers to buy them a round.
But they insist on buying drinks for him.
Go on tell us. Any hand-to-hand combat?
It's not like that, Liam tries to say,
his hands shaking beneath the table.
But he can see the pride in their eyes
when they look at him.

And he doesn't want to disappoint.
So he re tells this story he overheard
from an American Recon Marine.
In a jeep, no doors, clearing the way to Baghdad.
Cobras crossing in the sky.
Breathing through a gas mask.
Lads. We were just a group of sixty.
Spearheading the blitzkrieg
to save a city. Boom. Boom. Boom.
The baseline of bombs battering
beneath a burning sun.
In your ear a radio exploding.
The sound of all the engines.
Our AKs cracking like fireworks.
Bodies dropping around.
Buildings collapsing in the distance.
Just imagine, he says, watching them
all sitting transfixed. *I didn't sleep for three weeks,
not even for a moment. Fucking 'ell Liam*, they say.
*It sounds like Call of Duty that. You're a hero mate.
Doing us proud out over there. When are you going back?*
Liam stands, pats one on the shoulder,
and finishes off his pint. He's sweating.
His vision is starting to blur.
A couple of weeks, he says loosening his collar
and stepping towards the door.
He won't let it happen. Not here. Not with them.

VII

Clara leans her weight on the Stella handle,
hair long, dark and tangled.
A tatty t-shirt reading old bands that battled.
She pours herself a half
and watches from afar, as Liam leaves,
through the heavy wooden door.
She remembers him as a kid.
Little shit, full of beans, quick wit
just like his fists, a proper small town kid
with a sandpapered accent. Eyes bright blue.
Blond hair. Cute. She sips her beer
and sits down on the stool. Her back's giving in,
too many years of changing barrels.
She stretches it out and flicks over the TV channel.
Tipping Point. Catch Phrase. Mock the Week.
Re-runs of Top Gear. The same fold of old blokes
talking nothing but shite. She looks around,
see's the dust floating through the air, catching
the fruit machine's flashing lights.
She walks over to the Jukebox,
scrolls through the songs. Picks The Pogues
'Dirty Old Town' and closes her eyes.

It was her first dance with Connor. Back in '85,
when the only takeaway on these streets
was a chippy tea and at The Devonshire,

naked ladies danced for blokes sat at their seats.
She was 22, Connor was 30, lean but strong,
long brown hair, second hand Levi jeans,
with a Claddagh on his finger.
He rocked these black pair of Monkey Boots.
A proper Rocker. Soft as owt. Cheesy fucker.
But that didn't matter. He'd just taken over this place.
Within months, she'd moved in upstairs,
an old double mattress on a rickety bed
and a record player. Posters Blu-tacked
of all their favourite bands.
They used to watch the sunrise from their window
and sing songs about how the rays
kissed the rooftop of the mill.
They dreamt of growing old.
Building their little paradise bit by bit.
No kids. Neither wanted it.
And that's how they lived.
Summers back seeing his family
in Belfast, in a small, terraced house.
They'd spend their evenings sipping tea,
whilst huge iron gates got bolted every night
and kids hid in the shadows, dodging army trucks.
A city of hide and seek, where truth bites the body
like shrapnel from a gun. His Mum would tell
her stories about the women who hollowed out
their platform heels, making room for explosives,
or stood on top of trucks during the blockade of '69.
Demanding milk for their babies
as British tanks blocked the road,
whilst helicopters circled like falcons in the sky.
No food, she'd say. *The shops empty as a squaddies heart.*

Every year, they'd drive back through the hills,
slowing into corners, singing all their favourite songs.
She always wondered how it must feel for Connor,
driving back to where you live. But always leaving home.

The first thing Clara noticed
was how Connor lost the art of rolling cigarettes.
He just couldn't make it work.
Thumb knocking filter from the Rizla.
He started smoking straights, but then she noticed
how he began to mix the names of all their punters,
and pulled different pints to what they ordered.
He cracked opens bottles of Pedigree when they wanted
Stella. His speech became fragmented.
The Doctor told her one Monday morning,
Look it's come early.
Alzheimer's is a slow destruction
that creeps throughout the body.
There's nothing you can do.
Just hold his hand, until the end.
Her response at first was parties,
every other evening in the pub.
She booked in bands, dj's, stand ups,
anything to just make him smile.
She took photographs of everything.
Connor pouring a pint. Connor smoking outside.
Connor dancing. Connor laughing.
Connor having a good time. Because Connor is still alive.
But slowly people noticed. They'd pull her aside
and go *look, is Connor doing alright?*
There's an emptiness behind his eyes.
She would get angry, tell them he is doing just fine.

How dare they question her husband's health,
it's because he's working so hard, to make sure
they all have a good time. So she stopped the nights.
Slowed everything down. Turned off the lights.
Kept it quiet, until dust started to settle along the pool cues
and wooden stools stayed stacked up by the window;
even on a Friday night. She didn't care.
Her punters went elsewhere. Connor grew quiet.
Silent. He'd just sit and stare into himself.
Nurses came and went. They helped her with meals,
kept her sane, told her jokes, made her feel ok.
One thing she wouldn't let them do was put him in a home.
No-way. She'd snap like scissors, cutting the suggestion
from the air. *He stays here. With me. Until his final breath.*
It's funny, in the final year, the final weeks,
the only thing that would make him settle
was the songs they used to sing,
driving home back from Ireland.
So she played them on repeat.
Sat next to him. And there they could exist together
sitting in the same daydream.

VIII

Joe's standing in his kitchen.
It's two days until his fight. He drops
the tea bag into the mug and tenses his core.
Listens to the water boil. He stares out
the window into the light morning sky.
His toes curl on the cold tiles beneath
his feet. The leaves are rustling
from the morning breeze. A lone sparrow
is standing on the gate. His Mum is still
asleep upstairs. She's been working
double time. Early mornings. Late at night.
She has this cough that just won't leave
her chest. He hears it every time she rises
from her bed. The kettle clicks. He lifts
it up and pours the water into the mug,
and let's the bag settle for ten.
Then stirs it anti clockwise for eight
before adding milk. One sugar. Then carries
it up the stairs. *Mum*, he says, pressing his head
against her bedroom door.
Got a cup of tea for you.
He hears her stir. Cough twice.
Leaves it by the door. She says.
What time is it? 6.45, says Joe,
I'm going for a run.
Shouldn't you be getting ready for school?

No its study leave remember?
Joe heads down the stairs,
jumping over the creaky step.
He laces up his trainers,
and spends a moment stretching,
before clicking the latch of the door.
Morning runs. He loves them.
How everyone and everything still feel totally asleep.
The way the cold air drifts over his arms.
How the morning mist rises from the hills.
He starts slowly, climbing up and out of town.
Past the corner shop. The Kings Head,
The Old Inn pub where his grandad used
to drink. He feels his lungs starting to work.
He finds the old Roman road,
cuts through the trees. And lengthens out his stride.
Up here, he feels like the only man alive.
He looks left and sees his town below.
The sun rising from behind the terraced houses.
The long shadow cast from the mill.
He feels his body warming up.
His muscles, tendons, ligaments propelling
him with every step. All working in perfect
unison like a well-oiled machine.
He relaxes his shoulders and rolls up his sleeves.
He can't wait for the fight. He pictures it.
The referee holding up his arms. His name
ringing through the speakers. He's going
to win. No question. He can't wait to prove
all those teachers wrong. The way they think
he won't amount to anything. Who put
him in bottom set. Who say well done

for trying when he has failed another test.
He slows down, as the path becomes narrow
and filled with stones. He focuses on his breathing.
Just the other day the career advisor
pulled him into the office and sat him down in the small
plastic chair. *Let's not lie*, he laughed, looking straight
at Joe. *These GCSEs aren't looking good.*
But I've found something you might like.
What's that? replied Joe, trying not to roll his eyes.
The man put on a serious face and told Joe
about the Army. How to sign up for the infantry.
You don't need any GCSE's.
You just need to be young, strong, and fit.
Go off and see the world, he said.
Go travelling. It will be an adventure
of a life time. I don't know. Vlad has told me
I can start working at the Gym.
I think I'd rather do that.
But the careers officer laughed again.
Where's your ambition young man?
Go and fight for your country.
Make something of yourself.
Joe approaches the road,
that final comment banging around his head.

IX

Jessie watches an old couple in the corner.
They're sat at the table by the window.
The old man is hunchbacked,
with old green tattoos running up
his arm. He's dressed in a black t-shirt
with jogging bottoms and Clarks shoes.
The woman looks smarter, with a perm
and a long heavy dress.
Jessie can smell her perfume
from the other side of the room.
They're both eating slowly.
Their chips soaked in gravy. Neither talking much.
Jessie can't help but watch them sit in silence.
Imagine being with the same person for sixty
years. What would you have left to say?
She shakes her head.
I don't think I'll ever settle down,
she says, turning to face her dad,
who's standing in front of the counter,
an apron slung over his shoulder.
Not even with Dean? he asks.
Jessie shakes her head,
dips her chip into the ketchup
and licks her lips. *I've already told you.*
I don't fancy him.
But he fancies you, her dad replies.

I think he's nice. Kind of awkward.
Kind of cute. I like the way he looks at you.
Jessie shakes her head.
Her dad walks behind the counter.
Opens the till, starts counting the left over change.
On the radio Corinne Bailey Rae, 'Put Your Records On'
begins to play. Rain slides down the cafe window.
So how are you feeling about the move?
asks her dad, closing the till
and wiping a cloth along the counter.
Yeah, nods Jessie. *Alright I guess,*
she says, picking up her final chip.
Her dad watches her take a bite.
When they first moved here, Jessie was five.
The other kids made fun of her accent.
She would run and hide. At night she'd fall asleep
holding old pictures of her friends.
He goes back to wiping the counter.
Sings the chorus of the song beneath his breath.
Jessie watches as the old couple stand.
She goes over to take their plates.
Was everything ok? she asks.
Aye grand, the old man says.
We'll miss your Dad.
He makes the best sausage and mash around.
Jessie laughs, and smiles, watches as they head
out the door. *That could be you and Dean,*
her Dad says. *Long distance works, you know.*
Me and your Mum did it when she was working
over in Greece. Jessie smiles, picks up the plates.
Shakes her head. One day she'll tell her Dad
how she really feels. But not yet. *I've got to go,*

she says, opening the door.
It's Joe's fight tonight.

X

Everyone is hammered,
standing on their feet,
arms around each other's shoulders
singing 'Come on Eileen'.
Jessie looks up, shakes her head,
swirls the ice around her coke
and eyes up a group of blokes.
They're dressed in white shirts,
and fat ties with brown shoes
and have cocaine rolling round their eyes.

Joe's waiting in the corridor,
standing next to Vlad.
He can hear the crowd singing,
the floor vibrating. *Joe,* says Vlad,
placing his arm around
the boy's shoulder. *Just remember
what I always say. Stay focused.
Stay in control. Don't abandon that anger.
Just hold it in. Let it roar, when you know
it's your time to win.*

The music changes. The doors open.
Joe walks out.
Liam looks over his shoulder.
Closes one eye.
Tries to blink out the black dots

that are floating around him like flies.
Joe looks lean but strong.
Six pack chiselled into his adolescent skin.
It wasn't long ago when that was him,
training every other day
with Vlad down at the gym.

The bell rings. Joe steps forward.
He moves his feet. Shadows
his opponent's body. *This kid
looks scared*, he thinks working out
his opponent's reach. The kid swings,
but Joe moves back unbothered.
He steps in close, works the body.
Moves back out, takes a breath.
Side steps to the right,
then takes himself back to the left.

Jessie, says Dean placing
his arm over her shoulder.
What? says Jessie, turning her head
to face her oldest friend. His cheeks
are red, his eyes seem blank.
His breath stinks from everything
he's smoked and drunk.
Can I get you a drink? he says,
Jessie shakes her head.
Jessie, Dean says again.

Joe's in the corner, his back
leaning against the ropes.
He breathes in deep, puffs
out his cheeks, focuses
on the rhythm of his heart beat.
You've got this, Vlad says,
Move quick. Keep up your guard.
In this round you will feel
the moment. And when you do
just go with it.

Liam stands up, drains his glass
and moves through the crowd.
The yells. The bangs. The flashing lights.
He runs his hands through his hair.
Feels the grease slide between
his fingers tips. Everything is coming back.
The scorching sun. The Army boots.
The jeep out front. The narrow cobbled
streets. The tar melting beneath
a scorching sun.

The bell rings again and the kid
comes flying out from the ropes.
Throwing haymakers left and right.
Joe keeps his guard high, presses
his body close, takes a few blows,
before upper cutting him beneath
the chin. The kid sways back,
the crowd roars. Now's his moment.
He bites down on his lip,
puncturing the skin.

*

What the fuck, shouts Jessie,
pushing Dean away.
*Was it your brother's idea
to get me drunk? Just tip a few down
my neck. Get me loose.
When did you turn into such a dick
swinging loose lipped little shit?*
The worst thing is, she says,
pushing him again, *I thought
I could trust you.*

Liam pushes his body through
the door and feels the outside air hit
his face. A bus rolls past,
A car engine revs. *Not here*, he says.
Not in front of everyone.
He pulls his collar tight,
staggers left then right into the alley.
Two kids are smoking at the end.
Their faces covered. They watch him go
as he stumbles out onto the road.

Joe feels his knuckles crack the chin.
Liam stumbles through the door,
his muscles going stiff.
Jab. Cross. Hook. Cross.
Dean shakes his head.
Just let me buy you a drink,
he says again. Liam tries to stand,
but falls again,
blood dripping from his face.

Jab. Cross. Hook. Cross.
A ringing in his ears.
Jab. Cross. Hook. Cross.
A drum bangs somewhere in the distance.
Jab. Cross. Hook. Cross.
Liam blinks, feels the room fall
in and out of focus.
Jab. Cross. Hook. Cross.
Joe feels the arms of the referee
wrapped around his waist.
Jab. Cross. Hook. Cross.

XI

Dean's heading home past the flats,
where his brother is staying for a bit.
He rings the bell, but no one answers.
He must be asleep, he thinks.
He turns left, then right and cuts
through the park, and then on up the hill.
When he's at the top, he takes a moment,
looks at his town below. He can see Clara
ushering the final punters out of her pub.
He sees the bench, where he and Jessie
used to sit when they were young, counting
the cars as they passed. Guessing the names
of the drivers, making up stories of their past.
This town, he thinks, *is beautiful.*
The dark outline of the mill, the shadows
of the rolling hills that move down from the east
like steppingstones to the peaks.
The old Roman paths that run along the top.
The terraced houses. The cobbled streets.
The river flowing through. He lights up
a cigarette and feels the smoke
filling up his lungs. He exhales
into the air. Thinks of Jessie,
pictures the anger in her eyes.
Shakes his head. He flicks out
his cigarette, watches the embers

burn out on the ground, then glances up.
Sees an ambulance racing off
out of town like a firefly
shooting through the midnight sky.

Joe is standing alone in the changing room,
staring into the mirror. *What was that?* he thinks
studying his face. His eyes. His smile. His busted lip.
Vlad walks in smiling, arms wide open.
Bring it in, he says, *told you that you'd win.*
You need to take this moment in. Joe nods,
wipes the blood from his lip. Embraces Vlad.
What do you think I should do? says Joe.
Come work for me at the gym, says Vlad.
Me and Sarah can look after you.
Stay fit. Keep training.
You'll turn eighteen a year
before the next olympics.
We will get you funding.

XII

Back in the pub, Clara's behind the bar,
placing some food in a cardboard box,
as the twenty five year old versions
of Dean and Joe tip their pints back.
Once the box is full, she stands and pulls
herself a half, and lets the Guinness sit.
Her mind flicks back to when both those lads
were adolescent kids. Dean a nervous teen
always with a ciggie in his lips.
Joe was quiet. Determined. Hard as nails.
Ready to take from the world
what he thought was rightly his.
She smiles as Joe walks over.
Pours two pints of lager.
Nods to Joe as he passes
her a ten pound note,
then sits down on a wooden
stool as he walks away.
It's a shame, she thinks,
what happened to him.
A court case and everything.
But steroids are a dangerous thing.
She picks the paper up and glances at the letter
that's resting between the sports pages.
She re reads the figure.
That much for this? A cocktail bar

here? Five year's ago, she'd have laughed.
But now? This town's having a change of clientele.
People moving up with accents less
sandpapered than herself.
They drive nice cars, wear those quilted coats,
and don't say hello when they pass you in the street.
And they never come in here. No.
She just gets the same old blokes who sit
and nurse an ale. Play skittles out the back.
Smoke liquorice cigarettes in their stereotypical
farmer's flat caps. But they're getting older,
and the young uns prefer that new place
up at the top of town. She picks up the letter.
Let's her eyes scan the text.

This town's changed a bit, says Dean.
Aye it has. Says Joe. *It's been going down
the pan if you ask me. A bit of a pothole
to be honest. People are different now.
Are you still working at the gym?* asks Dean.
No mate, says Joe. *It closed a couple years back.
Some fella bought the whole Mill.
He's turning it into flats. And the boxing?*
asks Dean. Joe shakes his head
and sips his pint. *How is your brother doing?
What Liam?* Dean replies. *He's doing good.
Working for this charity now,
that's all about Mental health and PTSD.*
Joe nods and stands,
pushes the stool beneath the table.
Come on, he says. *Finish up. This place is dead.
There's a new Greene King up the road.*

Let's meet Jessie there. Dean nods again,
watches Joe place a cig behind his ear.
Dean necks his pint, picks up the glasses,
and carries them to the bar. *Nice one Clara,*
he says. *Good to see you Dean,* Clara replies,
and watches him turn and go out the door,
leaving her all alone. She picks up a mop,
starts humming that song her and her husband
used to sing. Maybe she should leave
and sell this place. She could use the money
to buy a house in that new estate,
just by the river, up the road, in that other town.

THANKYOUS

I'd like to thank the following people for all their help, support and conversations that have fed into this book. Crisby Brown, Tomas Thompson, Joshua Hallam, Anne Holloyway, Jamie Thrasivoulou, Polarbear, and Zoe Liz Turner. I'd also like to thank the students at Saint Benedicts School for the workshops right at the beginning of the writing, their thoughts and ideas can be seen throughout this text. Furthermore, a huge thanks to the King's College London Military Health Department, and the veterans they work with. Without all of you Liam wouldn't be the character he is.

A huge thanks to Cheryl Martin who mentored me so skillfully through the final drafts of the story. I think at times you believed in my writing more than I did, and to Roxanne Mores for the belief that this could be turned into a play. The amount of effort and work you have put in behind the scenes has been incredible.

Finally a huge thanks to Kate Ireland who I had the pleasure of sharing a stage with, and bringing these characters to life.

And of course thank you to Arts Council England, Contact and Derby Theatre for funding and commissioning this piece of writing.

ABOUT VERVE POETRY PRESS

Verve Poetry Press is a quite new and already prize-winning press that focused initially on meeting a local need in Birmingham - a need for the vibrant poetry scene here in Brum to find a way to present itself to the poetry world via publication. Co-founded by Stuart Bartholomew and Amerah Saleh, it now publishes poets from all corners of the UK - poets that speak to the city's varied and energetic qualities and will contribute to its many poetic stories.

Added to this is a colourful pamphlet series, many featuring poets who have performed at our sister festival - and a poetry show series which captures the magic of longer poetry performance pieces by festival alumni such as Polarbear, Matt Abbott and Imogen Stirling.

The press has been voted Most Innovative Publisher at the Saboteur Awards, and has won the Publisher's Award for Poetry Pamphlets at the Michael Marks Awards.

Like the festival, we strive to think about poetry in inclusive ways and embrace the multiplicity of approaches towards this glorious art.

www.vervepoetrypress.com
@VervePoetryPres
mail@vervepoetrypress.com